QUIET HOUR

Quiet Hour

Easy Ways to Reduce Stress and Relax in Nature

Heather Chase and Ken Beller

LTS Press

This program's content and activities are for informational purposes only and are not a substitute for professional medical advice. The authors and publisher assume no liability for accidents, injuries, or losses sustained by anyone who engages in the activities herein.

Copyright © 2024 by Heather Chase and Ken Beller

No part of this program may be reproduced or distributed without written approval from the publisher, except for uses permitted under fair use, such as in scholarly articles, critical reviews, or specific educational contexts. Valid licensees may replicate and distribute content for relevant educational activities.

LTS Press, P.O. Box 4165, Sedona, AZ 86340, info@ltspress.com, quiethour.org

ISBN: 978-0-9801382-4-5 (ebook) | ISBN: 978-0-9801382-5-2 (paperback)

Credits: cover: Heather Chase, p. viii: iStockphoto.com/Dinara Ilikaeva, p. 6: NPS, p. 7: iStockphoto.com/Sarah Braden, p. 7: Berry, Wendell. "The Peace of Wild Things." *Openings*, Harcourt, Brace & World, 1968, p. 8: Unsplash.com/ Ray Hennessy, p. 9: Unsplash.com/Ryan Jacobson, p. 10: Unsplash.com/Dharshatharan Jayatharan Aronan, p. 11: iStockphoto.com/Elena Goosen, p. 12: 123RF.com/oanwongteerayut, p. 27: 123RF.com/soloway

Contents

1. **INTRODUCTION** 1
   - Today's Noise and Stress Problem 2
   - An Appealing Solution 3
   - What Is Quiet Hour? 3
   - Benefits for You 4
   - Choosing a Location and Time 5
   - Handling Potential Challenges 6
   - Variations 6
     - Quiet Walk (or Other Outdoor Movement Activity) 7
     - Quiet Nature Art 8
     - Quiet Birdwatching (or Quiet Wildlife Watching) 9
     - Quiet Stargazing (or Quiet Moon Gazing or Quiet Cloud Gazing) 10
     - Quiet Movement 11
     - Quiet Mini-Retreat 12

2. **GUIDED EXPERIENCES** 13
   - Quiet Quarter-Hour 14
   - Quiet Half-Hour 15
   - Quiet Hour 16
   - Quiet Nature Art, Half-Hour 17
   - Quiet Nature Art, Hour 18
   - Quiet Birdwatching (or Wildlife Watching), Half-Hour 19
   - Quiet Birdwatching (or Wildlife Watching), Hour 20
   - Quiet Stargazing (or Moon or Cloud Gazing), Half-Hour 22
   - Quiet Stargazing (or Moon or Cloud Gazing), Hour 23
   - Quiet Movement, Half-Hour 24
   - Quiet Movement, Hour 26

3. **ADDITIONAL TOOLS** 29
   - Summary Cards 30
   - Micro-Experiences 31
   - Experience Plan, Log, and Reflections 32

1. INTRODUCTION

"For a time I rest in the grace of the world,
and am free."
—Wendell Berry

> 🔊 For audio recordings of this book, see the start of the **Guided Experiences** section.

Welcome to the Quiet Hour program. We're glad you're here. Here you'll discover a one-of-a-kind way to relax in nature. It's easy for everyone and can be done in any natural spot in as few as 15 minutes. This program has two main parts.

In the first part, you'll learn about Quiet Hour, the problem it helps solve, what Quiet Hour is, its benefits for you, suggestions for where and when to practice it, and for handling challenges that might happen.

In the second part, you'll experience the Quiet Hour process. You can listen along to it outdoors in your choice of three different lengths. Quiet Quarter-Hour, Quiet Half-Hour, or Hour. They all have the same steps, just different timing in each step.

Also, Quiet Quarter-Hour has fewer suggestions in each step. So let's begin by learning about Quiet Hour.

Today's Noise and Stress Problem

Rumbling traffic, blaring car alarms, pinging message alerts, upsetting twenty-four-hour news—today we are more bombarded with noise and stress than ever. We might try to ignore them or get used to them, but they take a bigger toll on us than we realize.

They are such a problem that the World Health Organization considers noise from traffic one of the worst environmental stressors for humans and calls stress the health epidemic of the twenty-first century.

Chronic noise causes stress, which in turn causes health problems. In fact, as published in the *American Journal of Industrial Medicine*, the *American Journal of Preventive Medicine*, and other sources, research shows that health risks of chronic noise exposure may include:

- Increased stress hormones
- Sleep disturbance
- Hearing impairment and tinnitus
- Triggers for people with post-traumatic stress disorder
- Changes in the immune system
- Hypertension and ischemic heart disease
- Diabetes
- Aggression, violence, and other anti-social behaviors
- Anxiety, depression, and other psychiatric disorders
- Birth defects
- Early death (In the EU, noise is considered a factor in ~10,000 deaths per year.)

An Appealing Solution

To reduce the impact of noise and stress, we might be tempted to hide out and wear ear plugs all the time. But there is a more appealing solution: quiet breaks in natural settings. Research study after study shows exposure to quiet and nature reduces stress. In fact, this has been confirmed in well over a hundred studies.

For example, research shows people who spend at least two hours in nature each week report significantly better health and well-being.

Publications by the American Heart Association, the American Psychological Association, and other sources reveal that some benefits of time in nature may include:

- Reduced stress/mental distress
- Decreased anxiety and depression
- Better mood/happiness
- Increased energy
- Improved heart health
- Increased positive social interactions
- Better self-esteem and concentration
- Increased memory, creativity, and work satisfaction
- Increased sense of belonging, meaning, and purpose in life
- Living longer

Plus, research indicates nature can meet psychological and emotional needs that are difficult to meet any other way.

But, in today's noisy, hectic, high-tech world, these benefits are out of reach for most people.

That's where Quiet Hour comes in. It can help bridge this gap and bring the benefits of quiet and nature to many more people.

What Is Quiet Hour?

It's an easy way to reduce stress and feel inner peace outside. Unlike most outdoor activities, it's not about learning a skill or information. It's about enjoying nature as a refuge from the pressures of modern life. It makes getting the benefits of quiet and nature easy.

The program is based on a simple, 4-step process of:

1. Center
2. Breathe
3. Notice
4. Appreciate

Woven into this process are nine techniques or influences that research indicates have a calming or uplifting effect, including:

1. Exposure to Nature
2. Hearing Quiet and Natural Sounds
3. Pausing Electronic Device Use
4. Earthing/Grounding (directly touching the earth)
5. Extended Exhale Breathing (breathing out longer than breathing in)
6. Sensory Awareness (noticing sensations)
7. Effortless Attention/Soft Fascination (being aware without having to concentrate)
8. Opportunities for Awe (chances to feel wonder or amazement)
9. Gratitude

A complete list of references is at quiethour.org/references.

Benefits for You

Quiet Hour is unique and easy to do. Basically, you follow some simple steps and nature does the rest.

- It's done seated or lying down.
- It's multi-sensory, so it's for people of all abilities, really everyone.
- You can practice it alone or with others, although the 60-minute version is best done with people ages 12 and older.
- It gives you a new way to experience nature, not by learning about it, playing in it, or exercising in it, but by feeling inner peace in it.
- While you might have felt this by chance on your own a few times, Quiet Hour gives you a structured, guided way to feel it often.
- It lets you turn any natural spot into a stress relief and mental wellness resource, where you can relax, replenish, and savor being alive on our wonderful planet.
- It's flexible, you can enjoy it in any natural spot, in any season, at any time of day or evening, and for either a quarter hour, half hour, or full hour.
- It's one of a kind and potentially transformative.
- It's a tool you can use often to manage stress and feel connected with nature for the rest of your life.

Choosing a Location and Time

You can practice Quiet Hour in any natural spot that's convenient for you.

This could be a park, a natural spot outside where you work, or your home's yard or balcony. If you can't get outdoors, you might try it near an open window facing a natural area. You can choose any natural spot, but here are some features to look for.

It's ideal if the spot is relatively quiet and natural. You'll have a better experience away from human-made noise like traffic and with more biodiversity than, say, a sports field. It's good if the spot is easy to get to.

Also, you could sit on the ground, but if you'd rather not, it's good if the spot has some seating, like a bench, or you could bring a folding chair. It's good if there's a restroom relatively close, so you can use it beforehand and be comfortable during the session.

It's an extra bonus if the spot is by water. Water tends to be soothing, attracts wildlife like birds, and makes the spot interesting. A spot doesn't have to have all these features, it's just nice if it does.

Do the best you can with what's near you. What if you have trouble finding a spot or you'd like to try a new one? You can search for natural spots on websites like alltrails.com, discovertheforest.org, and recreation.gov.

These locators are mostly in the US. If you're in another country, an online search should help you find similar locators for that country. As for timing, you can practice Quiet Hour at any time. It's especially nice at sunrise and sunset with their beautiful colors and changing conditions.

It's also nice to try it at different times of day or during different seasons. In terms of length, first you might start with quiet quarter hour, then if you like, over time you can gradually build up to the longer versions.

Again, they all have the same steps, just different timing in each step, and quiet quarter hour has fewer sub-steps. The most important thing is to do the process where and when it's comfortable and convenient for you.

That way, you'll be more likely to practice it often and enjoy the benefits long-term.

Handling Potential Challenges

During your Quiet Hour sessions, if challenges happen, feel free to pause the recording, handle them, then continue the recording when you're ready.

If the following specific challenges happen, handle them using your best judgment or these suggestions. If there is human-made background noise, it helps to realize that often stress comes from resisting what is.

To reduce that stress, we can relax our resistance to the sound and shift our focus to more pleasant natural sounds. Also, humans are part of nature too, and we can let their sounds blend with the other sounds.

If there is unpleasant weather, the suggestion is similar. Again, it helps to realize that often, stress comes from resisting what is. To reduce that stress, we can relax our resistance to the weather and shift our focus to something positive about it.

For example, wind can be uncomfortable, but also refreshing. Of course, if the noise or weather are extreme, you can stop and try again later. If you feel restless, feel free to stretch a bit. You're welcome to turn and face a different direction.

If you like, extend your exhale for a few more breaths. Maybe imagine you're a toddler, experiencing a place like this for the first time, with wonder and delight. Then continue where you were before the break.

If you lost time handling challenges and want to make it up, you can shorten the longest step. It's about two-thirds of the way through. It invites you to notice it all, and relax, and just be.

Variations

In addition to the standard Quiet Hour process, for variety, you might like to try some variations of it. Here's an overview of them. Full guidance for them are in the Guided Experiences section.

Quiet Walk
(or Other Outdoor Movement Activity)

This adds the Quiet Hour process to a walk or similar activity, to make the outing more relaxing and meaningful. It combines the wellness benefits of the Quiet Hour process and movement. You can listen along to a recording of the process before or after the activity, or half-way through the activity in an especially scenic spot.

If you listen along before or half-way through, then when you walk or do another activity, here are some things you might consider. You might continue being detached from devices and maintaining quiet. You might think about not moving in or through the natural area but moving with it—with natural things that are moving there and with nature. If there's any more stress you'd like to release, you might exhale, move, or shake it out of your body, like animals do after a stressful event—they shake it off. Or you might enjoy *getting to* breathe and move. Things like rocks don't get to, but you and animals do. Maybe enjoy this gift with animals, feeling alive with them.

There's no special recording for this. You can use the recording of your choice for Quiet Hour, Half-Hour, or Quarter-Hour.

Quiet Nature Art

This is a way of creating art in a natural area designed to be more relaxing and meaningful. It combines the mental wellness benefits of the Quiet Hour process and creativity.

The Quiet Hour process helps you get settled and connect with the area. Then, you can create something in response to the area. It's not about skills or the result. It's about reducing stress and connecting with nature by creating *with* it. It requires very few, or no, art supplies and no talent or expertise.

You can sketch or write a poem or a song with supplies like a thin sketchpad (or a couple sheets of blank paper and a clipboard) and a pencil with an eraser. Or you can take photos with a camera.

Or you can make temporary art with natural materials you find in the spot, like sand or small rocks. If you do that, please choose a spot that isn't too ecologically fragile and bring a camera to take a picture of your art before you return the materials.

Quiet Birdwatching
(or Quiet Wildlife Watching)

This is a way of watching birds (or wildlife) designed to be more relaxing and meaningful. It blends the mental wellness benefits of the Quiet Hour process and birdwatching (or wildlife watching).

It's not about analyzing birds (or wildlife) but enjoying them and reducing stress by watching them.

It's done seated and doesn't require any expertise or gear like binoculars, which are optional. It's best in a spot rich in birds or other wildlife, like near water or a birdbath, at a time when birds or other wildlife will likely be there.

Quiet Stargazing
(or Quiet Moon Gazing or Quiet Cloud Gazing)

This is a way of stargazing (or watching the moon or, in the daytime, clouds) designed to be more relaxing and meaningful. It blends the mental wellness benefits of the Quiet Hour process and sky gazing.

It's not about analyzing the sky and what's in it but enjoying them and reducing stress by watching them. It doesn't require any expertise or gear like telescopes, which are optional.

It's best in a spot with a good view of the sky.

It's especially nice during a meteor shower or new moon for stargazing, a full moon for moon gazing, or a day that's partly or mostly cloudy for cloud gazing.

You're welcome to bring a blanket, mat, or reclining lawn chair. For stargazing or moon gazing, to preserve your night vision, you might bring a red astronomy flashlight. For daytime cloud gazing, to protect your eyes, you might use sunglasses.

Quiet Movement

This is a way of gently moving designed to be more relaxing and meaningful. It blends the wellness benefits of the Quiet Hour process and movement.

It's not about fitness or flexibility but reducing stress and connecting with nature by breathing or gently moving *with* it. Instead of doing set moves at a set pace, you do your own breathing or movements, at your own pace.

It can be done seated and doesn't require any gear, fitness, special clothing, or expertise. It's best in a spot that will likely be breezy, has trees or plants likely to move in the breeze, and/or is rich in birds or other wildlife, like near water or a birdbath.

Quiet Mini-Retreat

This is a way to relax and connect with nature deeply over a few hours. First, you can do a Quiet Hour session or variation. Then, you can stay detached from devices and keep maintaining quiet while you have a picnic.

During the picnic, you can keep noticing sensations, including the sensations of eating. Maybe notice how your meal feels, looks, sounds (as you bite and chew), smells, and tastes.

Also, you can reflect on how nature contributed to your meal—like how sunlight, water, soil, etc. helped plants grow, which you're eating in some form. You might think about how they'll give you energy or become part of your body. So, nature is directly supporting your life. You might also reflect on how you have this in common with birds or other wildlife around you.

Then, after the picnic, you might do another Quiet Hour session or variation.

There's no special recording for this. You can use any of the Quiet Hour or variation recordings.

So that's what Quiet Hour and its variations are all about. In the rest of this program, you'll experience them. You can listen along to the recordings of them, in different lengths, in any natural spot. We hope you enjoy them.

2. GUIDED EXPERIENCES

> 🔊 Audio recordings of this book are at **quiethour.org/audios**

You can do the experiences with the audios above or the text below. In the text, notes in brackets are for clarity and aren't said in the audios. Also in the text, it's best to pause after each suggestion as appropriate, do the suggestion, then go to the next one.

Quiet Quarter-Hour

Welcome. Feel free to bring anything you might need for your safety or comfort to a natural spot.

[*Agreements*, ~1 min.] On the device you're listening with, it's best to close all other programs and apps and turn off all notifications and message alerts.

So you can hear the natural sounds around you, please listen to this with the device's main speaker or only one earbud, not both or headphones. It's also best to place the device screen side down, turn away from it, and don't use it for anything else during the session, unless something is urgent.

If you're with anyone else, it's best to agree not to talk during the session, unless something is urgent. Everything else in the session is optional.

[*Get Comfortable*, ~1.5 min.] You can sit up on something, on the ground, or lie down. If you like, you can rest your hands on the ground or take your shoes and socks off and rest your bare feet on the ground. Feel free to settle in and relax.

[*Center*, ~1.5 min.] Feel free to let everything else in your life pause. For now, you can let it all go. Here and now, you can rest.

[*Breathe*, ~1.5 min.] Now, you might become aware of your breathing. You might gently extend your exhale, like inhale 1, 2, 3, exhale 1, 2, 3, 4, 5. You can keep breathing this way on your own.

[*Notice—Feeling*, ~1.5 min.] You might notice what your body is feeling. Maybe feel your seat or the ground supporting you. Maybe feel the air.

[*Notice—Seeing*, ~1.5 min.] Feel free to notice what you're seeing. What do you see nearby? What do you see further away?

[*Notice—Hearing*, ~1.5 min.] You might notice what you're hearing. In between the sounds, can you hear quiet?

[*Notice—Smelling*, ~1.5 min.] You might notice what you're smelling. If there are some natural things beside you, feel free to smell them.

[*Notice—It All*, ~2 min.] Maybe notice it all together, the whole natural system here. Let your awareness open and expand. You can relax and just be.

[*Appreciate*, ~1.5 min.] Now, you might feel grateful for something here, maybe the fresh air or the quiet. Lastly, maybe appreciate yourself for taking time to do this process.

Well done.

Quiet Half-Hour

Welcome. Feel free to bring anything you might need for your safety or comfort to a natural spot.

[Agreements, ~1 min.] On the device you're listening with, it's best to close all other programs and apps and turn off all notifications and message alerts.

So you can hear the natural sounds around you, please listen to this with the device's main speaker or only one earbud, not both or headphones. It's also best to place the device screen side down, turn away from it, and don't use it for anything else during the session, unless something is urgent.

If you're with anyone else, it's best to agree not to talk during the session, unless something is urgent. Everything else in the session is optional.

[Get Comfortable, ~3 min.] You can sit up on something, on the ground, or lie down. If you like, you can rest your hands on the ground or take your shoes and socks off and rest your bare feet on the ground. Feel free to settle in and relax.

[Center, ~3 min.] Welcome to here and now. Feel free to let everything else in your life pause. For now, you can let it all go. Maybe imagine your stress evaporating into the air. Here and now, you can rest.

[Breathe, ~3 min.] Now, you might become aware of your breathing. You might gently extend your exhale, like inhale 1, 2, 3, exhale 1, 2, 3, 4, 5. Inhale 1, 2, 3, exhale 1, 2, 3, 4, 5. You can keep breathing this way on your own.

[Notice—Feeling, ~3 min.] You might notice what your body is feeling. Maybe feel your seat or the ground supporting you. Maybe feel the air. Or, if there are some natural things beside you, within arm's reach, feel free to feel them.

[Notice—Seeing, ~3 min.] Feel free to notice what you're seeing. What colors and objects are here? What do you see nearby? What do you see further away?

[Notice—Hearing, ~3 min.] You might notice what you're hearing. What are the main sounds? What are the quieter sounds? In between the sounds, can you hear quiet?

[Notice—Smelling, ~3 min.] You might notice what you're smelling. Maybe keep smelling the air. Or, if there are some natural things beside you, within arm's reach, feel free to smell them.

[Notice—It All, ~5 min.] Maybe notice it all together, the whole natural system here. Let your awareness open and expand. We'll be in this step longer than the others, so you can relax and just be. *[Pause ~3 min.]* If you like, can you relax 10% more?

[Appreciate, ~3 min.] Now, you might feel grateful for something here, maybe the fresh air or the quiet. You might appreciate it all, everything here that added to your experience. Lastly, maybe appreciate yourself for taking time to do this process.

Well done.

Quiet Hour

Welcome. Feel free to bring anything you might need for your safety or comfort to a natural spot.

[Agreements, ~2 min.] On the device you're listening with, it's best to close all other programs and apps and turn off all notifications and message alerts.

So you can hear the natural sounds around you, please listen to this with the device's main speaker or only one earbud, not both or headphones. It's also best to place the device screen side down, turn away from it, and don't use it for anything else during the session, unless something is urgent.

If you're with anyone else, it's best to agree not to talk during the session, unless something is urgent. Everything else in the session is optional.

[Get Comfortable, ~6 min.] You can sit up on something, on the ground, or lie down. If you like, you can rest your hands on the ground or take your shoes and socks off and rest your bare feet on the ground. Feel free to settle in and relax.

[Center, ~6 min.] Welcome to here and now. Feel free to let everything else in your life pause. For now, you can let it all go. Maybe imagine your stress evaporating into the air. Here and now, you can rest.

[Breathe, ~6 min.] Now, you might become aware of your breathing. You might gently extend your exhale, like inhale 1, 2, 3, exhale 1, 2, 3, 4, 5. Inhale 1, 2, 3, exhale 1, 2, 3, 4, 5. You can keep breathing this way on your own.

[Notice—Feeling, ~6 min.] You might notice what your body is feeling. Maybe feel your seat or the ground supporting you. Maybe feel the air. Or, if there are some natural things beside you, within arm's reach, feel free to feel them.

[Notice—Seeing, ~6 min.] Feel free to notice what you're seeing. What colors and objects are here? What do you see nearby? What do you see further away?

[Notice—Hearing, ~6 min.] You might notice what you're hearing. What are the main sounds? What are the quieter sounds? In between the sounds, can you hear quiet?

[Notice—Smelling, ~6 min.] You might notice what you're smelling. Maybe keep smelling the air. Or, if there are some natural things beside you, within arm's reach, feel free to smell them.

[Notice—It All, ~10 min.] Maybe notice it all together, the whole natural system here. Let your awareness open and expand. We'll be in this step longer than the others, so you can relax and just be. *[Pause ~7 min.]* If you like, can you relax 10% more?

[Appreciate, ~6 min.] Now, you might feel grateful for something here, maybe the fresh air or the quiet. You might appreciate it all, everything here that added to your experience. Lastly, maybe appreciate yourself for taking time to do this process.

Well done.

Quiet Nature Art, Half-Hour

Welcome. Feel free to bring anything you might need for your safety or comfort and art supplies or a camera to a natural spot.

[**Agreements**, ~1 min.] On the device you're listening with, it's best to close all other programs and apps and turn off all notifications and message alerts.

So you can hear the natural sounds around you, please listen to this with the device's main speaker or only one earbud, not both or headphones. It's also best to place the device screen side down, turn away from it, and don't use it for anything else during the session, unless something is urgent.

If you're with anyone else, it's best to agree not to talk during the session, unless something is urgent. Everything else in the session is optional.

Before creating art, you're welcome to settle in here.

[**Get Comfortable**, ~2 min.] You can sit up on something, on the ground, or lie down. If you like, you can rest your hands on the ground or take your shoes and socks off and rest your bare feet on the ground. Feel free to settle in and relax.

[**Center**, ~2 min.] Feel free to let everything else in your life pause. For now, you can let it all go. Here and now, you can rest.

[**Breathe**, ~2 min.] Now, you might become aware of your breathing. You might gently extend your exhale, like inhale 1, 2, 3, exhale 1, 2, 3, 4, 5. You can keep breathing this way on your own.

[**Notice—Feeling**, ~2 min.] You might notice what your body is feeling. Maybe feel your seat or the ground supporting you. Maybe feel the air.

[**Notice—Seeing**, ~2 min.] Feel free to notice what you're seeing. What do you see nearby? What do you see further away?

[**Notice—Hearing**, ~2 min.] You might notice what you're hearing. In between the sounds, can you hear quiet?

[**Notice—Smelling**, ~2 min.] You might notice what you're smelling. If there are some natural things beside you, feel free to smell them.

[**Notice—It All & Create**, ~13 min] Now that you've noticed nature's art, you're welcome to create your own. You might take nature photos, sketch, or write a poem or a song. Or, like nature's temporary art, like a sunrise, you can make temporary art with natural materials here. If you do that, please use things that are already loose, like sand or small rocks, so nothing gets damaged. You can "borrow" the materials, make your art, maybe take a picture of it, and, at the end, put the materials back.

Whatever you make, this is not about talent or the result. It's about reducing stress and connecting with nature by creating *with* it. You might think of nature as your art collaborator. This is between you and nature. You're welcome to begin.

The creating time has about 5 minutes left. You might start wrapping up.

Now, the creating time is up.

[*Appreciate*, ~2 min.] Now, you might feel grateful for something here, maybe the fresh air or the quiet. Lastly, maybe appreciate yourself for taking time to do this process.

If you "borrowed" natural materials, you're welcome to take a picture of your art and then return the materials to where you found them.

Well done.

Quiet Nature Art, Hour

Welcome. Feel free to bring anything you might need for your safety or comfort and art supplies or a camera to a natural spot.

[*Agreements*, ~1 min.] On the device you're listening with, it's best to close all other programs and apps and turn off all notifications and message alerts.

So you can hear the natural sounds around you, please listen to this with the device's main speaker or only one earbud, not both or headphones. It's also best to place the device screen side down, turn away from it, and don't use it for anything else during the session, unless something is urgent.

If you're with anyone else, it's best to agree not to talk during the session, unless something is urgent. Everything else in the session is optional.

Before creating art, you're welcome to settle in here.

[*Get Comfortable*, ~3 min.] You can sit up on something, on the ground, or lie down. If you like, you can rest your hands on the ground or take your shoes and socks off and rest your bare feet on the ground. Feel free to settle in and relax.

[*Center*, ~3 min.] Feel free to let everything else in your life pause. For now, you can let it all go. Here and now, you can rest.

[*Breathe*, ~3 min.] Now, you might become aware of your breathing. You might gently extend your exhale, like inhale 1, 2, 3, exhale 1, 2, 3, 4, 5. You can keep breathing this way on your own.

[*Notice—Feeling*, ~3 min.] You might notice what your body is feeling. Maybe feel your seat or the ground supporting you. Maybe feel the air.

[*Notice—Seeing*, ~3 min.] Feel free to notice what you're seeing. What do you see nearby? What do you see further away?

[*Notice—Hearing*, ~3 min.] You might notice what you're hearing. In between the sounds, can you hear quiet?

[*Notice—Smelling*, ~3 min.] You might notice what you're smelling. If there are some natural things beside you, feel free to smell them.

[*Notice—It All & Create*, ~34 min] Now that you've noticed nature's art, you're welcome to create your own. You might take nature photos, sketch, or write a poem or a song. Or, like nature's temporary art, like a sunrise, you can make temporary art with natural materials here. If you do that, please use things that are already loose, like sand or small rocks, so nothing gets damaged. You can "borrow" the materials, make your art, maybe take a picture of it, and, at the end, put the materials back.

Whatever you make, this is not about talent or the result. It's about reducing stress and connecting with nature by creating *with* it. You might think of nature as your art collaborator. This is between you and nature. You're welcome to begin.

The creating time is about half-way finished. You're doing great.

The creating time has about 5 minutes left. You might start wrapping up.

Now, the creating time is up.

[Appreciate, ~3 min.] Now, you might feel grateful for something here, maybe the fresh air or the quiet. Lastly, maybe appreciate yourself for taking time to do this process.

If you "borrowed" natural materials, you're welcome to take a picture of your art and then return the materials to where you found them.

Well done.

Quiet Birdwatching (or Wildlife Watching), Half-Hour

Welcome. Feel free to bring anything you might need for your safety or comfort to a natural spot.

[Agreements, ~1 min.] On the device you're listening with, it's best to close all other programs and apps and turn off all notifications and message alerts.

So you can hear the natural sounds around you, please listen to this with the device's main speaker or only one earbud, not both or headphones. It's also best to place the device screen side down, turn away from it, and don't use it for anything else during the session, unless something is urgent.

If you're with anyone else, it's best to agree not to talk during the session, unless something is urgent. Everything else in the session is optional.

Before turning your attention to the birds (or wildlife), you're welcome to settle in here.

[Get Comfortable, ~2 min.] You can sit up on something, on the ground, or lie down. If you like, you can rest your hands on the ground or take your shoes and socks off and rest your bare feet on the ground. Feel free to settle in and relax.

[Center, ~2 min.] Feel free to let everything else in your life pause. For now, you can let it all go. Here and now, you can rest.

[Breathe, ~2 min.] Now, you might become aware of your breathing. You might gently extend your exhale, like inhale 1, 2, 3, exhale 1, 2, 3, 4, 5. You can keep breathing this way on your own.

[Notice—Feeling, ~2 min.] You might notice what your body is feeling. Maybe feel your seat or the ground supporting you. Maybe feel the air.

[Notice—Seeing, ~2 min.] Feel free to notice what you're seeing. What do you see nearby? What do you see further away?

[Notice—Hearing, ~2 min.] You might notice what you're hearing. In between the sounds, can you hear quiet?

[Notice—Smelling, ~2 min.] You might notice what you're smelling. If there are some natural things beside you, feel free to smell them.

[Notice—Birds (or Wildlife), ~13 min.] You might notice some birds (or wildlife) here. Maybe don't strain to find them, identify them, or analyze them, but just enjoy them and *be with* them.

Now, if you'd like to release more stress, feel free to take some deep breaths and exhale the stress out, like birds flying away.

Now, as you are aware of them, could they also be aware of you? You might listen to any sounds they're making, like it's their music.

Now, you might think of them as your wild neighbors, fellow residents of the earth, or friends keeping you company.

Now, do they have a quality you'd like to feel? Maybe they're free. You're welcome to feel that freedom, breathing and expanding with it.

Now, feel free to breathe *with* them, sharing this air and this place with them… savoring this moment of being alive with them.

[Appreciate, ~2 min.] Now, you might feel grateful for something here, maybe the fresh air or the quiet. Lastly, maybe appreciate yourself for taking time to do this process.

If you "borrowed" natural materials, you're welcome to take a picture of your art and then return the materials to where you found them.

Well done.

Quiet Birdwatching (or Wildlife Watching), Hour

Welcome. Feel free to bring anything you might need for your safety or comfort to a natural spot.

[Agreements, ~1 min.] On the device you're listening with, it's best to close all other programs and apps and turn off all notifications and message alerts.

So you can hear the natural sounds around you, please listen to this with the device's main speaker or only one earbud, not both or headphones. It's also best to place the device screen side down, turn away from it, and don't use it for anything else during the session, unless something is urgent.

If you're with anyone else, it's best to agree not to talk during the session, unless something is urgent. Everything else in the session is optional.

Before turning your attention to the birds (or wildlife), you're welcome to settle in here.

[Get Comfortable, ~3 min.] You can sit up on something, on the ground, or lie down. If you like, you can rest your hands on the ground or take your shoes and socks off and rest your bare feet on the ground. Feel free to settle in and relax.

[Center, ~3 min.] Feel free to let everything else in your life pause. For now, you can let it all go. Here and now, you can rest.

[Breathe, ~3 min.] Now, you might become aware of your breathing. You might gently extend your exhale, like inhale 1, 2, 3, exhale 1, 2, 3, 4, 5. You can keep breathing this way on your own.

[Notice—Feeling, ~3 min.] You might notice what your body is feeling. Maybe feel your seat or the ground supporting you. Maybe feel the air.

[Notice—Seeing, ~3 min.] Feel free to notice what you're seeing. What do you see nearby? What do you see further away?

[Notice—Hearing, ~3 min.] You might notice what you're hearing. In between the sounds, can you hear quiet?

[Notice—Smelling, ~3 min.] You might notice what you're smelling. If there are some natural things beside you, feel free to smell them.

[Notice—Birds (or Wildlife), ~34 min.] You might notice some birds (or wildlife) here. Maybe don't strain to find them, identify them, or analyze them, but just enjoy them and *be with* them.

Now, if you'd like to release more stress, feel free to take some deep breaths and exhale the stress out, like birds flying away.

Now, as you are aware of them, could they also be aware of you? You might listen to any sounds they're making, like it's their music.

Now, you might think of them as your wild neighbors, fellow residents of the earth, or friends keeping you company.

Now, do they have a quality you'd like to feel? Maybe they're free. You're welcome to feel that freedom, breathing and expanding with it.

Now, feel free to breathe *with* them, sharing this air and this place with them... savoring this moment of being alive with them.

[Appreciate, ~3 min.] Now, you might feel grateful for something here, maybe the fresh air or the quiet. Lastly, maybe appreciate yourself for taking time to do this process.

Well done.

Quiet Stargazing (or Moon or Cloud Gazing), Half-Hour

Welcome. Feel free to bring anything you might need for your safety or comfort to a natural spot.

[*Agreements*, ~1 min.] On the device you're listening with, it's best to close all other programs and apps and turn off all notifications and message alerts.

So you can hear the natural sounds around you, please listen to this with the device's main speaker or only one earbud, not both or headphones. It's also best to place the device screen side down, turn away from it, and don't use it for anything else during the session, unless something is urgent.

If you're with anyone else, it's best to agree not to talk during the session, unless something is urgent. Everything else in the session is optional.

Before turning your attention to the sky, you're welcome to settle in here.

[*Get Comfortable*, ~2 min.] You can sit up on something, on the ground, or lie down. If you like, you can rest your hands on the ground or take your shoes and socks off and rest your bare feet on the ground. Feel free to settle in and relax.

[*Center*, ~2 min.] Feel free to let everything else in your life pause. For now, you can let it all go. Here and now, you can rest.

[*Breathe*, ~2 min.] Now, you might become aware of your breathing. You might gently extend your exhale, like inhale 1, 2, 3, exhale 1, 2, 3, 4, 5. You can keep breathing this way on your own.

[*Notice—Feeling*, ~2 min.] You might notice what your body is feeling. Maybe feel your seat or the ground supporting you. Maybe feel the air.

[*Notice—Seeing*, ~2 min.] Feel free to notice what you're seeing. What do you see nearby? What do you see further away?

[*Notice—Hearing*, ~2 min.] You might notice what you're hearing. In between the sounds, can you hear quiet?

[*Notice—Smelling*, ~2 min.] You might notice what you're smelling. If there are some natural things beside you, feel free to smell them.

[*Notice—The Sky*, ~13 min.] Now, you're welcome to stay as you are or lean back or lie down. You might notice the sky and natural things in it. Maybe don't strain to find them, identify them, or analyze them, but just enjoy them and *be with* them.

Now, if you'd like to release more stress, feel free to take some deep breaths and exhale the stress out into space.

Now, can you sense the earth gently hugging you to it through gravity, holding you lightly yet securely? You're welcome to soften into that stability.

Now, you might notice being in the earth's atmosphere, the bubble around our planet where conditions are just right to support life. Can you sense some of that support?

Now, you might notice natural things in the sky. Maybe think of them as your cosmic neighbors or friends keeping you company.

Now, you might notice the infinite space. Does it have a quality you'd like to feel? Maybe it's spacious. You're welcome to feel that spaciousness, breathing and expanding with it…savoring this moment of being alive in the universe…resting in the mystery of it all.

[Appreciate, ~2 min.] Now, you might feel grateful for something here, maybe the fresh air or the quiet. Lastly, maybe appreciate yourself for taking time to do this process.

Well done.

Quiet Stargazing (or Moon or Cloud Gazing), Hour

Welcome. Feel free to bring anything you might need for your safety or comfort to a natural spot.

[Agreements, ~1 min.] On the device you're listening with, it's best to close all other programs and apps and turn off all notifications and message alerts.

So you can hear the natural sounds around you, please listen to this with the device's main speaker or only one earbud, not both or headphones. It's also best to place the device screen side down, turn away from it, and don't use it for anything else during the session, unless something is urgent.

If you're with anyone else, it's best to agree not to talk during the session, unless something is urgent. Everything else in the session is optional.

Before turning your attention to the birds (or wildlife), you're welcome to settle in here.

[Get Comfortable, ~3 min.] You can sit up on something, on the ground, or lie down. If you like, you can rest your hands on the ground or take your shoes and socks off and rest your bare feet on the ground. Feel free to settle in and relax.

[Center, ~3 min.] Feel free to let everything else in your life pause. For now, you can let it all go. Here and now, you can rest.

[Breathe, ~3 min.] Now, you might become aware of your breathing. You might gently extend your exhale, like inhale 1, 2, 3, exhale 1, 2, 3, 4, 5. You can keep breathing this way on your own.

[Notice—Feeling, ~3 min.] You might notice what your body is feeling. Maybe feel your seat or the ground supporting you. Maybe feel the air.

[Notice—Seeing, ~3 min.] Feel free to notice what you're seeing. What do you see nearby? What do you see further away?

[Notice—Hearing, ~3 min.] You might notice what you're hearing. In between the sounds, can you hear quiet?

[Notice—Smelling, ~3 min.] You might notice what you're smelling. If there are some natural things beside you, feel free to smell them.

[Notice—The Sky, ~34 min.] Now, you're welcome to stay as you are or lean back or lie down. You might notice the sky and natural things in it. Maybe don't strain to find them, identify them, or analyze them, but just enjoy them and *be with* them.

Now, if you'd like to release more stress, feel free to take some deep breaths and exhale the stress out into space.

Now, can you sense the earth gently hugging you to it through gravity, holding you lightly yet securely? You're welcome to soften into that stability.

Now, you might notice being in the earth's atmosphere, the bubble around our planet where conditions are just right to support life. Can you sense some of that support?

Now, you might notice natural things in the sky. Maybe think of them as your cosmic neighbors or friends keeping you company.

Now, you might notice the infinite space. Does it have a quality you'd like to feel? Maybe it's spacious. You're welcome to feel that spaciousness, breathing and expanding with it…savoring this moment of being alive in the universe…resting in the mystery of it all.

[Appreciate, ~3 min.] Now, you might feel grateful for something here, maybe the fresh air or the quiet. Lastly, maybe appreciate yourself for taking time to do this process.

Well done.

Quiet Movement, Half-Hour

Welcome. Feel free to bring anything you might need for your safety or comfort to a natural spot.

[Agreements, ~1 min.] On the device you're listening with, it's best to close all other programs and apps and turn off all notifications and message alerts.

So you can hear the natural sounds around you, please listen to this with the device's main speaker or only one earbud, not both or headphones. It's also best to place the device screen side down, turn away from it, and don't use it for anything else during the session, unless something is urgent.

If you're with anyone else, it's best to agree not to talk during the session, unless something is urgent. Everything else in the session is optional.

Before moving, you're welcome to settle in here.

[Get Comfortable, ~2 min.] You can sit up on something, on the ground, or lie down. If you like, you can rest your hands on the ground or take

your shoes and socks off and rest your bare feet on the ground. Feel free to settle in and relax.

[Center, ~2 min.] Feel free to let everything else in your life pause. For now, you can let it all go. Here and now, you can rest.

[Breathe, ~2 min.] Now, you might become aware of your breathing. You might gently extend your exhale, like inhale 1, 2, 3, exhale 1, 2, 3, 4, 5. You can keep breathing this way on your own.

[Notice—Feeling, ~2 min.] You might notice what your body is feeling. Maybe feel your seat or the ground supporting you. Maybe feel the air.

[Notice—Seeing, ~2 min.] Feel free to notice what you're seeing. What do you see nearby? What do you see further away?

[Notice—Hearing, ~2 min.] You might notice what you're hearing. In between the sounds, can you hear quiet?

[Notice—Smelling, ~2 min.] You might notice what you're smelling. If there are some natural things beside you, feel free to smell them.

[Notice—Movement, ~13 min.] Now, you're welcome to stay as you are or stand. You might notice one part of nature here. Feel free to breathe, make a shape with your body, lightly stretch, or gently move like it, or how it might move at other times. Maybe don't worry about how you look—just breathe and comfortably move *with* this part. This is between you and nature. Maybe let this feel good, like an animal waking up, yawning or stretching.

Good. You're welcome to keep going with this part of nature or switch to another one anytime. Maybe think of it as your practice partner or friend doing this with you.

Good. You can keep going with this part or switch to another one. If there's any more stress you'd like to release, maybe exhale, move, or shake it out of your body, like animals do after a stressful event—they shake it off.

Good. You can keep going with this part or switch to another one. Can you enjoy *getting to* breathe and move? Things like rocks don't get to, but you and animals do. Can you enjoy this gift with animals, feeling alive with them?

Good. As you breathe or move, you might think of opening space in your body, to feel freer and absorb any goodness that's here.

Good. Now, you're welcome to slow down and notice any energy or aliveness in your body... savoring this moment of feeling alive with nature.

[Appreciate, ~2 min.] Now, you might feel grateful for something here, maybe the fresh air or the quiet. Lastly, maybe appreciate yourself for taking time to do this process.

Well done.

Quiet Movement, Hour

Welcome. Feel free to bring anything you might need for your safety or comfort to a natural spot.

[**Agreements**, *~1 min.*] On the device you're listening with, it's best to close all other programs and apps and turn off all notifications and message alerts.

So you can hear the natural sounds around you, please listen to this with the device's main speaker or only one earbud, not both or headphones. It's also best to place the device screen side down, turn away from it, and don't use it for anything else during the session, unless something is urgent.

If you're with anyone else, it's best to agree not to talk during the session, unless something is urgent. Everything else in the session is optional.

Before moving, your welcome to settle in here.

[**Get Comfortable**, *~3 min.*] You can sit up on something, on the ground, or lie down. If you like, you can rest your hands on the ground or take your shoes and socks off and rest your bare feet on the ground. Feel free to settle in and relax.

[**Center**, *~3 min.*] Feel free to let everything else in your life pause. For now, you can let it all go. Here and now, you can rest.

[**Breathe**, *~3 min.*] Now, you might become aware of your breathing. You might gently extend your exhale, like inhale 1, 2, 3, exhale 1, 2, 3, 4, 5. You can keep breathing this way on your own.

[**Notice—Feeling**, *~3 min.*] You might notice what your body is feeling. Maybe feel your seat or the ground supporting you. Maybe feel the air.

[**Notice—Seeing**, *~3 min.*] Feel free to notice what you're seeing. What do you see nearby? What do you see further away?

[**Notice—Hearing**, *~3 min.*] You might notice what you're hearing. In between the sounds, can you hear quiet?

[**Notice—Smelling**, *~3 min.*] You might notice what you're smelling. If there are some natural things beside you, feel free to smell them.

[**Notice—Movement**, *~34 min.*] Now, you're welcome to stay as you are or stand. You might notice one part of nature here. Feel free to breathe, make a shape with your body, lightly stretch, or gently move like it, or how it might move at other times. Maybe don't worry about how you look—just breathe and comfortably move *with* this part. This is between you and nature. Maybe let this feel good, like an animal waking up, yawning or stretching.

Good. You're welcome to keep going with this part of nature or switch to another one anytime. Maybe think of it as your practice partner or friend doing this with you.

Good. You can keep going with this part or switch to another one. If there's any more stress you'd like to release, maybe exhale, move, or shake it out of your body, like animals do after a stressful event—they shake it off.

Good. You can keep going with this part or switch to another one. Can you enjoy *getting to* breathe and move? Things like rocks don't get to, but you and animals do. Can you enjoy this gift with animals, feeling alive with them?

Good. As you breathe or move, you might think of opening space in your body, to feel freer and absorb any goodness that's here.

Good. Now, you're welcome to slow down and notice any energy or aliveness in your body… savoring this moment of feeling alive with nature.

[Appreciate, ~3 min.] Now, you might feel grateful for something here, maybe the fresh air or the quiet. Lastly, maybe appreciate yourself for taking time to do this process.

If you "borrowed" natural materials, you're welcome to take a picture of your art and then return the materials to where you found them.

Well done.

3. ADDITIONAL TOOLS

Fillable/printable versions of these tools are at **quiethour.org/audios**

Summary Cards

As an alternative to doing sessions with the audio, you're welcome to do them with these cards. They summarize the main steps of the process. On the Quiet Hour Variations card, the "Notice—Birds, Sky, etc." step means notice the focus of the variation you choose (birds, the sky, movement, etc.)

To make the cards, print or photocopy them on cardstock and cut them out. For one double-sided card, glue them together back-to-back. To make it more durable, you can laminate it.

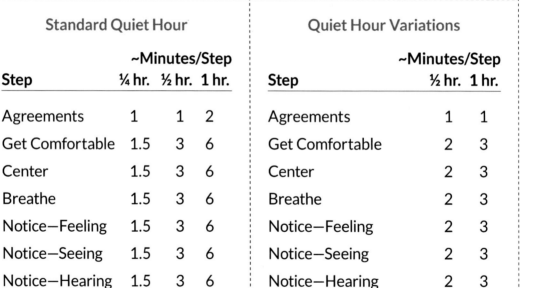

Standard Quiet Hour				Quiet Hour Variations		
	~Minutes/Step				~Minutes/Step	
Step	¼ hr.	½ hr.	1 hr.	Step	½ hr.	1 hr.
Agreements	1	1	2	Agreements	1	1
Get Comfortable	1.5	3	6	Get Comfortable	2	3
Center	1.5	3	6	Center	2	3
Breathe	1.5	3	6	Breathe	2	3
Notice—Feeling	1.5	3	6	Notice—Feeling	2	3
Notice—Seeing	1.5	3	6	Notice—Seeing	2	3
Notice—Hearing	1.5	3	6	Notice—Hearing	2	3
Notice—Smelling	1.5	3	6	Notice—Smelling	2	3
Notice—It All	2	5	10	Notice-Birds, Sky, etc.	13	34
Appreciate	1.5	3	6	Appreciate	2	3

Micro-Experiences

When you can't do full Quiet Hour sessions, you might do parts of them for a moment. Micro-experiences like these can be quick de-stressors and nature check-ins to enhance your everyday life. Below are some ideas for them.

- Opening a window or stepping outside and taking a few breaths of fresh air
- For a few breaths, extending your exhale (e.g., inhaling for 3, exhaling for 5)
- Pausing human-made sounds and listening for quiet or natural sounds
- Looking out a window and noticing part of nature, even if just the sky
- In a somewhat natural spot, pausing to just be
- Noticing part of nature moving (e.g., branches swaying in the breeze)
- Noticing any tension in your body and, if you like, relaxing 10% more
- Feeling grateful for part of nature (e.g., plant-made oxygen you're breathing)
- Noticing if you can see, or hear, any birds
- Facing the sky, exhaling stress out into space, imagining the stress evaporating
- Shaking off some stress, like animals do

When I could do some of these and/or more ideas I have:

Experience Plan

If you'd like help planning a session, you're welcome to fill in this page.

1. I hope this session helps me (e.g., de-stress):

2. The Quiet Hour version I'd like to do (e.g., Quiet Half-Hour):

3. A good location for the session (e.g., my patio):

4. A good day and time for the session (e.g., Sunday afternoon):

5. A good length for the session (e.g., half-hour):

6. Anyone I'd like/need to involve (e.g., a relative to join me):

7. Anything I need for my unique situation (e.g., wear sunglasses):

8. Any unique challenge that might happen (e.g., pollen allergy flare-up):

9. A way I could handle this challenge (e.g., take allergy medicine before):

Experience Log

If you'd like help doing a series of sessions, you're welcome to fill in this log. After each session, you can fill in a row with when and where you did the session, the version you did (Quiet Half-Hour, Quiet Walk, etc.), and how it was.

To help me (e.g., de-stress): _____, I intend to do at least this version (e.g.,

Quiet Half-Hour): _____ this often (e.g., once a week): _____.

	When	Where	Version and How it Was
1			
2			
3			
4			
5			
6			
7			
8			
9			
10			
11			
12			
13			
14			

	When	Where	Version and How it Was
15			
16			
17			
18			
19			
20			
21			
22			
23			
24			
25			
26			
27			
28			
29			
30			
31			
32			
33			

	When	Where	Version and How it Was
34			
35			
36			
37			
38			
39			
40			
41			
41			
43			
44			
45			
46			
47			
48			
49			
50			
51			
52			

Experience Reflections

After a session (any version), or a series of sessions, you're welcome to reflect on it here.

I enjoyed this.	Yes ○	No ○
It was relaxing.	Yes ○	No ○
It helped me feel closer to nature.	Yes ○	No ○
I feel better now than before doing this.	Yes ○	No ○

Reflections:

Thank you for trying Quiet Hour. Hopefully, it has made a positive difference for you. Did you notice every session is different depending on what nature is doing? Considering that, and other things you might have liked about this, we hope you'll keep enjoying the experiences often. May they continue to help you feel inner peace outside.

Made in the USA
Las Vegas, NV
24 March 2025